# VICTORIAN FASHIONS

## A PICTORIAL ARCHIVE

Selected and Arranged by
Carol Belanger Grafton

Dover Publications, Inc.
MINEOLA, NEW YORK

## Copyright

## Bibliographical Note

*Victorian Fashions: A Pictorial Archive* is a new work, first published by Dover Publications, Inc., in 1999.

## DOVER *Pictorial Archive* SERIES

## Library of Congress Cataloging-in-Publication Data

Grafton, Carol Belanger.
  Victorian fashions : a pictorial archive / selected and arranged by Carol Belanger Grafton.
       p.      cm. — (Dover pictorial archive series)
  ISBN 0-486-40221-5 (pbk.)
  1. Costume—History—19th century—Pictorial works. I. Title. II. Series.
GT596.G72      1999
391'.009'034—dc21                                98-49148
                                                    CIP


Manufactured in the United States of America
Dover Publications, Inc., 31 East 2nd Street, Mineola, N.Y. 11501

# NOTE

Culled from rare periodicals and catalogs, these Victorian fashions reflect the changing styles of women's clothing from 1855 to the turn of the century. Elaborate collars, decorative edgings, lace, and ornately trimmed hats were ever-present in Victorian clothing. This book, comprising an array of late-19th-century women's wear essentials such as bustles, balloon sleeves, and tight corsets, spans fifty years of fashion.

The sources of these illustrations include major American, British, and European fashion periodicals of the times: *Godey's Lady's Book, Peterson's Magazine, Harper's Bazar, La Mode Illustrée, Salon de la Mode, Dames et des Demoiselles, L'Art et la Mode, Der Bazar,* and others, as well as such general interest periodicals as *Frank Leslie's Ladies' Magazine* and *Harper's Weekly.* Many illustrations come from trade catalogs such as *The Standard Designer.*

The plates included here are arranged chronologically. An invaluable resource, this collection of illustrations tracks the history and progress of Victorian fashion.

1895

1863 ❦ 3

4 ᔕ 1863

1864 ❦ 5

14 ✦ 1871

1874 ❧ 17

*1886*   35

54 ⚜ 1801

1894   73

94 ❦ 1898

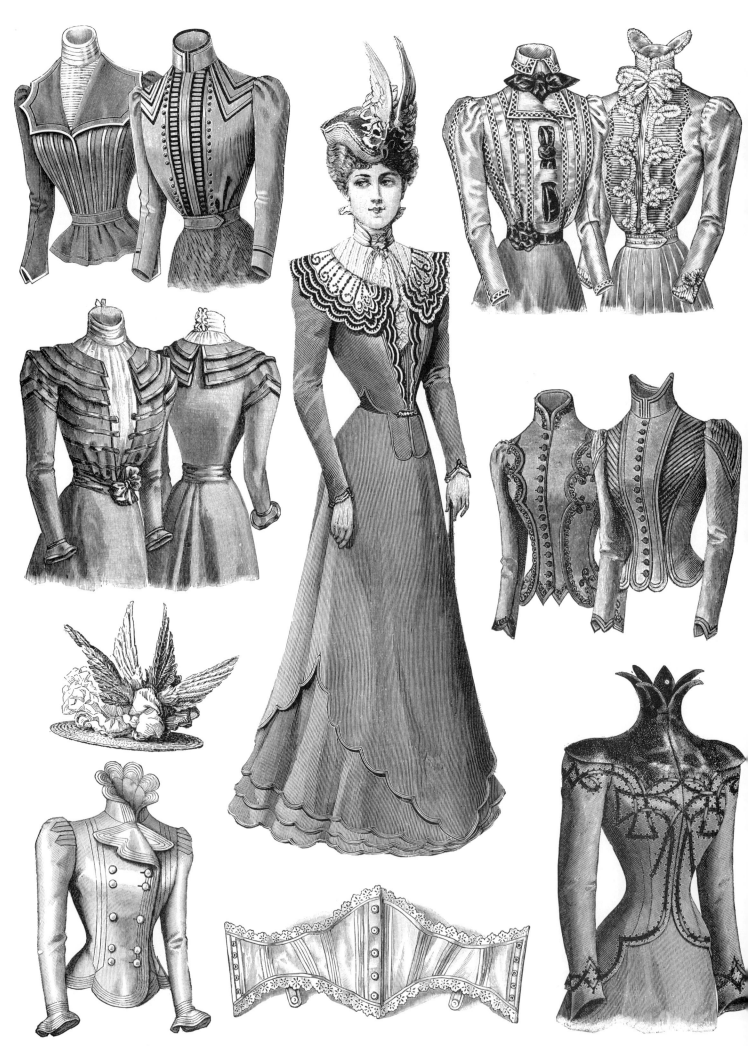